D1601175

THE
PARROT
TRAINING
HANDBOOK

THE
PARROT
TRAINING
HANDBOOK

By Jennifer Warshaw
Cover Art
By Debbie Silverman
Illustrations
By Kara Hubbard

Published by
Parrot Press
San Jose, California

First Printing 1990
Second Printing 1990
Third Printing 1991

Although the author has made a rigorous attempt to exhaustively research and clarify all advice offered herein, no liability will be assumed due to omissions, inaccuracies, or misinterpretation.

Warshaw, Jennifer
    The Parrot Training Handbook
    Parrot Press
    1. Parrot Training - Behavior, Intelligence of
    I. Warshaw, Jennifer   II. Title

Library of Congress Card Catalogue Number: 90-90255

ISBN 0-9626724-0-8

DEDICATION

*To all of the kindred souls who look
beyond the difficulty of living with pet birds
and cherish their magnificence.*

TABLE OF CONTENTS

PREFACE

I wrote this book out of a need that I perceived for a clear, well-organized book on the subject of bird training. As a writer I was disappointed with the books I found on the subject. Though I am not a professional bird trainer, I have trained horses and dogs professionally and I have successfully tamed and trained my own pet parrots.

During the years that I have worked with animals, I have seen many very accomplished trainers who have difficulty teaching the training process. These people are expert trainers who achieve excellent results. The problem is that they have so internalized the training process, they forget to explain the individual steps involved. They have completely lost the perspective of the beginner.

Approaching bird training with a beginner's mind and armed with the conviction that I would be successful (based on my previous experience with other animals), I carefully observed the steps that I took. With patience and many mistakes, I discovered and recorded methods for training and taming birds that anyone can employ successfully. This book is the product of trial and error, extensive research, and experience. I wrote this book as I struggled to understand and train my own birds. I have learned a great deal in this process, and my curiosity has been fueled by it. My goal is to help parrot owners understand their pets more clearly, so that they can live with them more happily.   I hope it is clear, simple, and fun to use.

HOW TO USE THIS BOOK

This book is laid out so that a beginning trainer with a wild-caught bird can successfully tame and trick-train their bird. Scan each section and determine where your bird is in the taming and training process. Make sure that your bird is ready to progress to the next level of training before attempting it. Training is a series of carefully calculated steps that, if taken in sequence, are much easier and more effective.

This book is designed to be used like a cookbook or instruction manual. The book can lay flat in front of you while you train your parrot, so that if you get confused or forget a step, you can stop and reread the text.

The print in this book is larger than in most books so that people who wear reading glasses may not have to wear them while conducting their training sessions. I have yet to meet a parrot that will leave my glasses on my face.

Each trick has a similar layout. The following page shows what each trick looks like and how the information should be used.

TRICK NAME

Needs: A list of what you'll need to prepare
before beginning the training session.

Training time: This is designed to give you
an idea of how long the average bird will be
attentive at a particular level of training. It
also limits the amount of time you should
spend on certain tricks that are highly
stressful to the parrot.

DESCRIPTION
*This section will give a description of the trick and
any special goals you'll want to keep in mind.*

1 Each step in the trick is clearly separated
from the next. You must learn to pace your
bird and have it master each step before
going on to the next one. It will be clear
when the bird understands one step of the
trick, and quickly responds with the desired
behavior. It will not be unusual for the bird
to only master one step per session. Don't
rush training.

2 You can expect to train your bird its first
complete trick within your first seven
sessions.

NOTE TO THE NOVICE TRAINER

Training is not "controlling" an animal's behavior, it is communication in a structured relationship with an animal. This is both a very fine line and a very important one. I don't want to give the impression that animals never need to be controlled. However, I strongly believe that communicating with an animal instead of controlling it will result in a happier, healthier, more trainable animal.

Whether you plan to train your bird to make it a movie star, a neighborhood attraction, or just a happier, more enjoyable pet, training done properly, will improve your relationship with your bird.

TRAINING IS COMMUNICATION...

I remember, when I was first learning to train animals, how miserable my attempts to produce the desired behaviors were. I have worked with young people and adults, teaching them to train animals, and it is always frustrating for them at first. But as a person begins to give an animal credit for its intellect and emotions, genuine communication between the animal and trainer occurs. This communication greatly increases the success of training.

I imagine the animal's experience of training to be like having someone drive up alongside you on the freeway and point at your back tire. It's nerve wracking trying to figure out what could possibly be wrong as you try to make sense of a complete stranger's hand signals. I picture myself as the wildly gesticulating motorist trying to get through to an animal as we begin our training relationship. I keep this image in mind, to aid me in maintaining patience and empathy with an animal throughout the early sessions.

TRAINING IS PAYING ATTENTION...

The finest animal trainers I have known all have had a few traits in common: they care about their animals, they are consistent and patient, and they concentrate on what they are doing. Because all of these traits are important to successful animal training, I would like to elaborate on each of them.

CARING for an animal means concern for its emotions, well being, and respect for its individuality. It means not forcing an animal to perform behaviors that are beyond its trust level, and not allowing the animal to become willful and headstrong. Just like parenting-- firm but caring.

CONSISTENCY means careful thought about a training session before it begins. Decide on the cues and bridges (more on this later) you will use before beginning the session. Don't reward your parrot for an incorrect behavior, and do not reward your parrot for a behavior when he wasn't given the cue to perform it. Patience means appreciating what little progress you will make with certain birds. Patience means keeping training sessions short at first and never abusing your bird's attention span. Patience means keeping your temper with a bird who is willful. And by the way, some birds will not or cannot be trained, but these are the exceptions.

CONCENTRATION means watching your bird

attentively and rewarding the small steps he takes towards performing the behavior you want. Rewards must be immediate, so that a connection between the behavior and reward can be established in the parrot's mind.

Concentration means that your body language, voice, and behavior are consistent with what you want the bird to do. I find that a good way to keep my concentration on the training session is to picture the animal performing the behavior we are working on in my mind. In this way, I keep my attention on the task at hand more efficiently. There are some who believe that animals "see" these mental pictures. I don't know if this is true, perhaps it's just body language, but it works!

San José, California
January, 1990

Taming is the first step in training. The taming process you will use depends on the type of bird you have. If you own (or suspect that you own) a wild-caught bird, the taming process will be much more demanding than if your bird is a domestically bred, hand-raised, baby.

Hand raised babies, are bred in the United States and fed from the first few days of life by a highly skilled human being. These babies have no fear of humans and can be handled from the first day they are brought home. But, keep handling to a minimum at first, let the baby get used to being in its cage and feeding itself. As you see the hand fed baby begin to crack seed and find its own water dish, you can allow it out of its cage to be with the family more often.

Protect the trusting nature of your hand-fed baby by showing people, especially children, how to handle it properly. A bird is not a pet for a child. Until children demonstrate real concern for a bird's needs, they should only be allowed brief, supervised play time with the bird.

While hand-raised birds are usually eager to interact with people, and will react to your hand by trying to "feed" from it, wild-caught birds have usually not had a very good experience with humans. As babies, wild-caught birds may have watched as their parents were killed or wounded. The baby is then taken from the nest, stuffed into a cage, and roughly hand fed at a quarantine station. A wild-caught bird, hand fed at a quarantine station, will be sold as a hand-raised baby. These wild-caught, hand-fed babies are rarely as trusting as domestically hand raised youngsters.

If you are the owner of a wild-caught bird who you would describe as vicious, take heart. I know that you can tame this bird, with care and patience.

Though it is almost always possible to train a wild-caught bird (and they are preferred by most professional trainers because they are generally more reliable as performers), I feel it is important to understand the ordeal that a wild-caught bird has been through before you begin taming it. I am personally opposed to importation methods. Mortality statistics

for imported birds are sickeningly high (one study
estimated that 100 macaws die for each 1 pet bird
that successfully acclimates to a new home*). If you
are already the owner of an imported bird, please
take the time neccessary to tame it and to let it know
that it is safe, and wanted, in its new family.

*Source: California State Humane Association, "The High
Cost of a Bird in the Hand," C.H.A.I.N. Letter, Fall 1988.

Because I believe that understanding and compas-
sion are cornerstones of successful taming, I'll explain some common methods of capturing wild
parrots. To capture a wild parrot, importers may:
injure or kill the parents and take the young from
the nest, mass capture flocks of parrots with thin
nylon net, shoot birds in the wing, or use a sticky
substance painted on branches so that when a parrot
lands, he is a "sitting duck" waiting to be ripped
from the branch. Captured birds are then packed
into a crate with 20-100 other birds and shipped to
quarantine stations. Some birds die from fright,
some from the heat, some from starvation or thirst.
The birds that do survive must witness this carnage.
In 1988 an estimated 34 million of these birds did
not survive the trip into the United States.

Taming wild-caught birds may require
spending long periods of time with them in a room
where they have freedom to be away from you. Take
their cage into the bathroom (or other appropriate
room) and close the door. Leave some seeds or fruit
(a red apple for instance) outside of the cage. Each
day move this food closer to yourself, as a lure for
the bird to approach you. Talk to the bird in the
most soothing voice possible, and never raise your
voice. If you have a good singing voice, lullabies are
a wonderful method for calming birds. Try not to
approach your wild-caught bird first, let it make the
first move.

It may take a long time, day after day, week after
week, of sitting on the floor (where you are less
threatening), before your bird can raise his courage
to approach you. Anthropologists speed up the
procees of trust-building through the use of imitation. Watch your bird, being careful not to stare
(this is aggressive behavior), and imitate its behavior.
Talking or singing soothingly to the bird will also
help him become acclimated to you. Once the bird
is accepting your presence (calm when you are near),

you must begin to handle the bird. Any bird worth its feathers will attempt to bluff you out of getting near it by snapping at you. If this frightens you, wrap a towel around one hand, and gently deflect the bird's beak with your protected hand while you touch and caress its feet and body with the other. Yes, you may get bitten, but moving slowly and surely will not arouse a vicious bite from a bird who has been allowed to gain some trust in you. You may also begin by using a stick for the bird to perch on. Slowly move your hand up the stick, closer to the bird, until the bird is perching on the stick, with your hand touching its feet. This will be very stressful for the wild-caught bird and you should start by spending no more than five minutes handling him. Slowly increase the length of the sessions. Once the bird allows contact, progress to hand taming.

Although taming is a long, sometimes boring, process, it's rewarding for both the bird and the trainer. I keep my interaction with a new, traumatized bird to a minimum for the first few weeks, and then place it's cage where I can talk to it occasionally. I have discovered that if I delay handling the bird for a month or more, the bird has already developed some curiosity, and the taming process progresses more quickly.

After everything an imported bird has been through, taming is the process of saying "Welcome home" to an intelligent creature who is capable of affection.

NOTE: The bird may have to go through this process with each member of the family who wants to handle him. A bird shows fear by "displaying", or ruffling up the feathers on its head and moving away from the object it is afraid of. If the bird shows this type of behavior with someone, have that person go through the taming or trust building process with the bird.

TRUST BUILDING METHODS

Trust is the foundation upon which any training regimen should be built. When training a parrot, first spend time building the parrot's confidence in you. Once you have a parrot's trust, getting their attention is much simpler. Birds are social animals who will be anxious for whatever time and contact they can have with their trusted friends. Birds get very lonely and display psychic disorders, like feather plucking, if they do not have a close, trusting relationship.

Trust-building can be done in many ways. Here are a few methods to use with tame birds to get them ready for training:

NOTE: It isn't necessary to use all of these steps with every bird. As soon as your bird is anxious to be with you, confidently hopping onto your hand, and/or comfortably looking you in the eye, you are ready to begin training.

ONE

When you have 15-30 minutes to spend with your bird, sit down with it in a relatively quiet place (in front of the T.V. is o.k. for most birds). Start with scratching and ruffling the feathers at the back of its head. After a few minutes of this, some parrots will allow you to scratch anywhere on their body. Take it slowly, move from the head to the top of the neck, speaking softly to the parrot.

Do not try to force your bird to allow more contact than he is comfortable with-- coax him to let you scratch under his wings, his legs, stroke his feet, etc. An essential element to gaining a bird's trust is letting the bird dictate how much, how soon. Most birds will forget they were ever squeamish about letting you handle their wings, legs, and tail. This exercise also makes wing and nail clipping a breeze.

TWO

Share food or spoon feed. Most birds enjoy having a taste of whatever you are having, and will put their trust in a person who feeds them. Spoon feeding will have the same affect on some birds as hand-raising. Spoon feeding can be done with the bird's favorite treat, or anything you both enjoy. Maintain eye contact (but don't stare down a shy bird) and speak softly to the bird while feeding it.

THREE

So that the bird does not associate you with fear and pain, have someone else, a veterinarian or groomer, handle unpleasant tasks like nail and wing clipping.

FOUR

Imitate the bird's gestures and sounds, especially if the bird calls to you when you leave the room. Imitation is used by most wild animal trainers, to gain an animal's trust. If the bird is ignoring you, shutting its eyes, or looking away as soon as you make eye contact, it is shy and afraid. Make a game out of this behavior by slowly shutting your eyes or turning your head, letting the bird be the one looking at you. This can be a marvelous game for increasing a bird's confidence.

FIVE

Rescue the bird from a threatening situation. If your bird somehow gets into trouble, get it out of harm's way. This method will not be useful unless you can calmly accept the possibility of getting bitten. A scared bird is unpredictable, if this frightens you don't rescue your bird without a towel to place over its head.

INTRODUCTION TO TRAINING

A well-trained parrot is one of the most entertaining pets a person can live with. Once a parrot has learned new ways to get attention it will probably become a ham. I have watched trick-trained parrots desperately going through their entire repertoire of tricks again and again to get the attention of a group of people who were watching another bird go through its paces.

THINK LIKE A PARROT...

Empathy is one of the most important tools that you'll use in taming and training your parrot. I believe that birds experience emotions somewhat like our own. I have seen my favorite parrot mad, frightened, jealous, content, rowdy, and happy.

When a parrot is behaving badly, snapping at someone for example, I do two things. First, I discipline him for snapping by isolating him from me. And second, I try to figure out why he is biting and cure the cause. Biting is one of the most common problems with pet birds. You'll find suggestions for cutting down on biting in the following section on behavior conditioning.

You must take several preliminary steps before you begin to trick-train your parrot. Unless you properly prepare yourself and your bird for trick-training, your results will be mixed.

A quiet place: Set up your training headquarters where where you'll have the least distractions--if possible, choose a room that can be closed off for the entire session. Many people find the bathroom ideal, though mirrors can be a real distraction for some parrots. Don't forget, your jewelry and watch are a distraction. Remove them.

The perch: A T-stand or simple perch is the best way to keep your parrot's attention focused on the training session. If you do not already own a T-stand, the back of a chair can be used as long as the bird can grip the chair back comfortably. Do not have toys or dishes on the training perch that can distract the bird.

Treat acclimation: The training reward must be a small size that can be swallowed quickly. I use shelled peanuts, (broken in half), shelled sunflower seeds, or pieces of fruit for overweight birds.

If your parrot does not already have a favorite treat, you can acclimate him by adding 1-2 tablespoons of the intended treat to his food for approximately two weeks. Begin to watch for signs that he has eaten his special treat before his regular food. Now comes the nasty part. Eliminate the treat from his diet. He will not be given this food except during training sessions. When a treat acclimated bird, who knows a few tricks, sees his treats, he will usually do one of his tricks to try to get one.

If your parrot does not seem interested in the treat or the training sessions, it can help to remove all food from its cage for 1-4 hours before the training session. Experiment with the amount of time it takes to peak your own bird's appetite.

NOTE: Sunflower seeds have a great deal of oil in them, this means two things: they are fattening (so are peanuts) and they spoil quickly. I buy shelled, unsalted sunflower seeds from a health food store; human, food-grade seeds are much less likely to have sat in storage, and cause less digestive problems for your bird.

Bridging: A *bridge* is a sound cue that lets your bird know he has done what you wanted and is about to get a reward. The use of a bridge is essential in getting your bird to associate his reward with his behavior. Training without a bridge is considerably slower than otherwise.

Clickers and other Bridges: Many animal trainers make use of clickers as a bridge. I have seen them used, and think they are wonderful, but I prefer to train my birds with one hand free (One hand is at the ready with a treat, at all times).

I prefer to use a verbal bridge, not only because I naturally respond with an immediate "good," when my birds behave, but also because I have a tendency to misplace little things like clickers. I use "Good!" in an enthusiastic, pleasant tone. I know a trainer who says "Smart Bird!" which some of her birds amusingly repeat. The most important criteria for choosing a successful bridge is that the word comes naturally to you. Your bridge does not have to be a word, any short, distinct, sound will do.

Cues: A wonderful thing about parrot training is that some birds will not only perform the desired behavior but they will also repeat the verbal cue. I always take this possibility into consideration when deciding what cue I will use.

However, if you are training your bird with the hope of getting him to perform professionally, always progress to the use of non-verbal hand cues in the latter stages of training.

Discipline: Unlike many other animals, birds do not understand physical discipline. Birds are rarely aggressive in the wild--the act of fluffing up their feathers (called "showing" or "displaying") is about as aggressive as they get. Therefore, I do not strike a bird at any time, it confuses them and causes them to lose faith in you. However, if you are quick, you can attempt to restrain a bird from biting or other undesired behavior while saying "BAD" or "NO". If an undesirable outcome occurs for the bird, like isolation or restricted movement, the bird will begin to understand the general meaning of "NO" or "BAD". Consistency is the key.

The most important consideration in choosing a discipline for your bird, is that it suits the bird's personality. An effective discipline for a wild-caught bird is being placed on the floor, where it will feel insecure. For a hand-raised baby this will not work and the worst fate is usually isolation. Individual birds are different. You may already know what the best discipline for your bird is--as long as it is not frightening for the bird, use it.

NOTE: When using your voice to convey displeasure, try to have a friend listen to see if your voice is too loud, or threatening. Don't shout.

PARROT HOLD

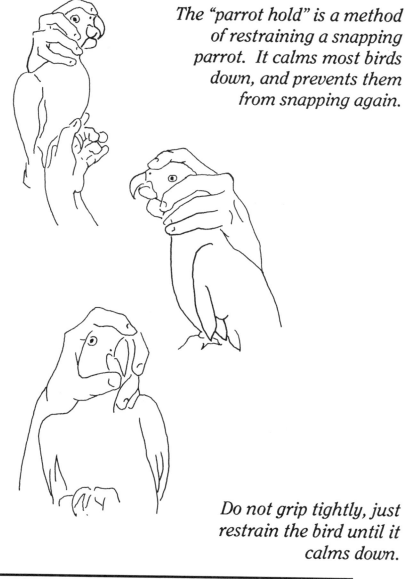

The "parrot hold" is a method of restraining a snapping parrot. It calms most birds down, and prevents them from snapping again.

Do not grip tightly, just restrain the bird until it calms down.

BEHAVIOR CONDITIONING

This section covers behaviors that can be conditioned, such as proper hand taming and potty training.

This section also covers methods for eradicating bad habits common to birds such as biting and screaming.

Look over this section and work on behaviors that you want your bird to perform (or not to perform) before beginning trick training.

Warning:
Allow a new pet to acclimate to its new home for at least a month before beginning taming or training. Training can be very stressful.

21

POTTY TRAINING

NEEDS: Newspaper, Trash Can or Litter Tray
           Reward
           Bridge
           Cue

DESCRIPTION

Few people realize that their bird can be potty trained. Potty training is perhaps the most individualistic of bird behaviors to condition. This is not a quick behavior to condition, but it is well worth the effort.

Although the directions below include a reward, most birds do not require bribing to perform this behavior on cue. There are birds who will defecate "on command" and others who will learn to notify you when they feel the need to go.

1   While playing with your bird, wait for it to show signs of needing to defecate. Birds will differ in the signs they exhibit, some drop their tail and wiggle back and forth, others stay still with a fixed stare. Some birds run around nervously, and I'm sure there are other behaviors that I haven't observed.

2 As your bird indicates its need to go, do something to distract it, such as getting up, saying "Wait a minute," and taking the bird over to the receptacle you have decided to use-- perhaps a piece of newspaper placed on the floor. Be consistent with the receptacle you use, it is part of the conditioned response.

3 Place the bird on, or in, the potty you have provided and cue it to go. Once the parrot evacuates, bridge and reward. Repeat this conditioning at least once a day. If you are lucky, your parrot will begin to notify you of its needs by announcing its cue, so choose something you'll want to hear in mixed company. Several birds I have seen and heard of have developed this behavior.

NOTE: Uh, Oh! is a cute cue for potty training and it is as inoffensive as can be when company is over. Even a potty-trained parrot will sometimes have an accident. How hard the bird will try get to its potty depends on the bird and the circumstances.

DEALING WITH BITING

When a pet bird bites me, I find it depressing. I take it personally and feel rejected. I walk away from the bird, my finger still hurting, and I feel confused and dejected. I think everyone feels that way. Time and experience have shown me that I can eradicate a significant amount of biting with patience and trust building.

WHY DO BIRDS BITE?

No one can be certain of the answer to this question, since we really can't be sure of the conclusions we draw from experience. But certain things seem to work with most birds to decrease biting.

There are very few birds that will never bite you. There are two bite-like behaviors in birds, one is biting and the other is the bird's use of its beak as a tool. A parrot will use its beak as a third "claw", in order to climb or catch its balance and to explore unfamiliar objects. This type of beak use is not considered biting, but a bird can learn how much pressure to use with you. Simply let the bird know when it hurts with a simple, "ouch" while pulling your hand away.

Real biting is a much different behavior. Birds bite in self-defense, terror or anger. When you say that you don't want your bird to bite, you are saying that you don't want him to become mad, playful, or frightened. A bite is usually your parrot's way of saying, "Hey! Slow down a bit!" This does not mean that I condone biting, but, *birds bite for a reason*. When a bird I have worked with bites at me, it is more like a nip than a bite. I believe that I am not often bitten severely because I stop and try to figure out what is bothering the bird before continuing. Usually he is off balance, rowdy, tired of the session, or feels the need to control my handling of him.

WHAT TO DO

To cut down on biting behavior, begin to notice when your parrot bites the most. I can't deal with all of the causes of biting, but I can demonstrate the way to go about problem solving with a parrot.

Does the bird bite when getting onto your hand?
> You may not have trained him how to get onto your hand confidently. The bird is using his beak for balance and security. The Hand Taming section will show you how to train

your parrot to get on your hand confidently.
I advise working on this behavior first, until
you have it mastered.

Another possible cause for biting is that your
bird does not yet have enough trust in you.
Take a few steps back, and begin with some of
the trust building methods described in the
last section. Make all of the bird's contact
with you positive. Hand feed him his favorite
foods, ruffle the feathers at the back of his
neck, sing to him, and let him decide when
he is ready to leave his territory and spend
time with you. It may take several months of
pampering him (leave wing and nail clipping
to the vet/groomer) before he'll trust you
enough to allow hand taming and trick
training.

Is he biting one member of the family exclusively?
Does this member of the family have a loud
voice, are they smaller, or very physically
different from you? Do they seem nervous
with the bird? Birds are very cautious
creatures. In the wild, trust is not an asset.

Birds learn slowly to put aside their instinct for caution. I recommend the taming exercise for this person. (And perhaps calming down that person first, *animals sense fear*).

People who are unfamilliar with birds commonly offer their finger, for the bird to "smell" as they would with an unfamilliar dog. Birds have a very poor sense of smell, but do have a sensory center at the tip of their beak, this is why they always test new things with their beaks. Let strangers interact with your bird by giving it a treat or by gently running their finger along the top of its beak.

Is the parrot biting everyone but his favorite person?
This is a tough one that takes some commitment to get rid of. I'll bet that the person reading this book is the bird's favorite person, and that brings up an interesting point. The other family members need to understand how much time and love have gone into developing the relationship

you have with the bird. The bird has probably bonded to the favored person and sees itself protecting its mate. The most appropriate punishment for this type of biting behavior in a bird is isolation from his beloved (you). It will take self discipline to put him in his cage every single time he is hostile to a family member, but it is the only way to teach the bird some self discipline. His favorite person should put him away, so that he doesn't associate the other family members with the punishment. Leave him in his cage for 10-20 minutes and then let him have another chance to come out and behave.

NOTE: The parrot's cage will have to be moved out of the family area while this behavior is going on. His favorite person can also gently close the bird's beak and say, "Bad," in a very dissaproving voice while taking him to his cage. Patience and a certain tolerance for being bitten without reacting too harshly will allow you to significantly reduce your bird's tendency to bite. Always deal systematically and empathetically when teaching your parrot new behaviors. If patience and empathy are used, you will find your parrot a joy to handle and happy to spend time with you.

ABOUT WEARING GLOVES

Some trainers recommend against wearing gloves to handle a biter. The theory is that it reminds imported birds of their first contact with humans. I believe that you should not subject yourself to severe biting, and that you can acclimate a bird to ignore a pair of gloves. If you own a wild-caught bird, you can wash a pair of gloves thoroughly and place them in the cage where the bird can get used to them. You can even place a treat in the palm of one the gloves while it is in the bird's cage.

Once the bird has stopped biting, stop wearing the gloves during handling.

SCREAMING

Screaming is one of the more annoying habits a pet parrot can acquire. Unfortunately, it is a natural behavior for many parrots--a way of expressing their anger, happiness, and declaring their presence to the world. Following are two methods of curbing screaming.

NOTE: Whatever you do, don't succumb to temptation and yell, "Be quiet!" at the bird, he may think you want to make a contest out of it.

SQUIRT BOTTLES

Although I do not like to use them for general
discipline, squirt bottles are excellent for curbing
screaming. Aim for the body, not the head, and use
only a few squirts. If it doesn't work right away, try
something else, so that you don't antagonize the bird.
Antagonizing a bird will jeopardize the training relationship you are working so hard on. If it works, be
consistent and leave the squirt bottle where your bird
can see it.

ISOLATION/COVERING THE CAGE

Removing the bird from the center of activity is
another way of dealing with screaming. For this
method to work, you must be consistent in removing
the bird from the center of activity when he begins
to scream. You may want to rig the cage cover so
that it can be easily lowered when the bird starts
screaming. If your bird is allowed to be out on a
playground, you must return him to his cage, which
needs to be placed away from the main activity of the
household. Allow him to come back out when he
has quieted down and remained quiet for a few minutes.

HAND TAMING

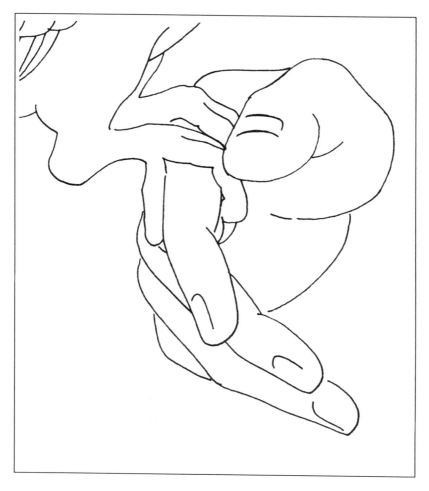

Training your parrot to calmly sit still on your hand is one of the most important behaviors you will teach your parrot to perform. This behavior seems simple, but for some birds there are many obstacles to overcome.

Needs: No treats, unless absolutely necessary
Reward with a head scratch
Cue
Bridge

 Lesson Time: 5-15 minutes depending on the bird's attention span

DESCRIPTION

The ability to get onto your hand calmly is essential for your bird's safety. I often have to rescue a bird from a dangerous situation (or from soiling something with droppings), and the ability to put my hand in front of the bird and say "Up" immediately reorientated the bird, and saved many upsets. I enjoy a chorus of "Up, Up, Up!" when I enter the bird room. I have also seen "Going up!" used, so that it sounds like an elevator operator, it's adorable to see a bird saying this as it is being lifted off of its perch.

Unless your bird is highly resistant, don't allow it to expect a reward for this behavior. This behavior is obedience and safety related (i.e., for the birds own good) and should evolve into a conditioned response (as opposed to a trick). Many experienced

bird trainers feel that birds are too selfish to do something just because you want them to. I have encountered birds like this, but I strongly recommend that you try to evoke this behavior without treats first. It's annoying to have to carry treats with you every time you want or need to move your bird.

1   For most birds it is important not to start hand taming from within the cage. If you cannot get your bird out, open the cage door and wait until it comes to the door. A bird can be dangerous when it is protecting its "territory".

2   Hold your hand against the bird's chest so that it can step up onto the knuckles of your index finger and the crook of your thumb. Apply slight pressure to coax the bird onto your hand while using your verbal cue.

If the bird snaps at you, speak soothingly and keep your hand at the bird's chest with gentle pressure (wear gloves if the bird is really bad). I say something to calm the bird, such as, "It's o.k., up!" And persist. Allowing a bird to not perform this behavior because of biting is a poor way to begin your training relationship. Stay calm, keep trying.

3 Once the bird is on your hand, gently close your thumb over its feet. The bird will not like it and will attempt to get its foot on top of your thumb, but continue to replace your thumb gently on top of the bird's feet. Teaching a bird to accept your thumb lying over its feet will begin to remind you of thumb wrestling, but be patient. Soon the bird will accept this contact. Later, if you are carrying the bird around and it attempts to fly away, you can restrain the bird for its own safety with a slight pressure from your thumb (place your free hand in front of the bird's chest as it tries to flee to keep it upright).

NOTE: You can prevent a bird from biting you by holding a pencil or other slim object in one hand to the hand that is being offered for perching by placing the pencil/object between the birds beak and your hand. After a few days you will find that simply holding the object will prevent the bird from attempting to nip your hand.

HAND TAMING—LESSON TWO

Needs: No treats, unless absolutely necessary
Reward with a head scratch
Cue
Bridge

 Lesson Time: 5-15 minutes depending on the bird's attention span

DESCRIPTION
Once your bird is confidently hopping onto your hand, the second step in hand taming is having the bird calmly sit on your hand. Many birds will attempt to climb up to your shoulder or fly off of your hand. A bird needs to stay on your hand as a simple, and safe, method of transportation. I find it comforting that I can get a sick bird to sit calmly on my hand for a trip to the vet, rather than further stressing him by using a carrier, or manhandling him.

1 Once your bird is on your hand, he will probably attempt to climb up your arm. Do not allow the bird to climb up to your shoulder. He must learn to sit calmly on your hand. Use your free hand to block the bird's progress up your arm--and if necessary, let him perch on your free hand.

2 Continue replacing the bird on the crook of your hand each time it attempts to climb up your arm. Gently place your thumb over the bird's toes. Each time the bird sits calmly for a few seconds, bridge and reward.

3 In this behavior, unlike the others, the bridge remains constant, i.e., "good", while the reward will be removed once the bird has learned how to get onto your hand and sit quietly. A bird can learn this behavior without receiving any reward (other than being out of its cage with you). Attempt to condition this behavior without a reward, but if you feel one is needed, use it.

If you choose to let your bird sit on your shoulder, place him there from your hand, giving him another verbal cue (e.g., "on the shoulder") while doing so. Letting him climb up your arm only erases everything you have just taught him.

NOTE: It is important to remain calm and firm with the bird during the lesson. If you raise your voice or grab at him, he will get too excited or frightened to make much progress.

THE NEXT STEP

Once your bird has learned this behavior you can comfortably and safely transport him or trick train him anywhere. It is usually simpler to keep a bird's attention when the bird is on a T-stand or simple perch, but let your bird graduate to doing his tricks from your hand so you can take the show on the road.

Now that your parrot has learned the proper way to get onto your hand and sit quietly, be sure that other family members or handlers don't allow the bird to break the rules. The sign on the following page can be posted in the bird room, to save confusing the trained birds and erasing their training.
I recommend copying it and posting it.

NOTICE

These birds are in training
and will be confused
and frightened
by improper handling.

PLEASE ...
ask for instructions
before handling

TRICK TRAINING

Trick training, will turn into play time once your parrot learns the ropes. You will use the same bridges and rewards for each trick. This first section contains beginning behaviors that you can teach your parrot. Master at least two of the beginning tricks before going on to intermediate tricks. Once your parrot has learned that he can earn a treat, get attention, and make you happy with him, his attention span and ability to learn tricks will improve.

Trick training can fall into two categories. The first is a learned behavior where the bird will perform an acquired behavior like riding a bicycle on cue. The second type of behavior is referred to as innovative behavior. An innovative behavior is one that your bird does naturally that amuses you. You can reward your bird for this behavior to encourage it, or shape the behavior into a trick.

REMINDERS

1   Use small, quickly eaten foods such as shelled seeds. Have the food readily available.

2	Conduct the training sessions daily, twice a day if possible. If things are going poorly, end the session early and on a good note.
3	Behaviors will take varying times to learn, depending on the rapport between the trainer and the bird.
4	If the bird gets nervous or frightened, slow down and calm the bird. Sitting on the floor with the bird can be an excellent method.
5	Decide on your cues, bridges, rewards, and punishments before beginning a session.
6	Be consistent.

How to tell if your bird is getting bored:

- Not interested in the reward
- Dropping the reward
- Reluctant or unwilling to perform learned behaviors
- Nervous or aggressive behavior such as beak wiping or snapping

If any of these things occur, get your bird to do one more simple behavior, bridge, reward and end the session, praising the bird. Abusing your bird's attention span will make him antagonistic towards training sessions.

If your bird becomes antagonistic to the training sessions, there are a few things you can try:

- Change the training treat
- Have a friend observe the training session to see if your gestures or tone of voice are frightening the bird
- Change the training time
- Shorten the training sessions
- Slow down, go back to the previous step in the trick or simpler behaviors
- Remove all food bowls from the bird's cage for 1-4 hours before the training session (a hungry bird is more attentive)

NOTE: I do not recommend the "starvation" methods endorsed by many respected trainers. A common recomendation is to allow free-feeding for only one hour per day. It does assure a dependable, attentive bird, but I think this method is both inhumane and unnecessary.

WAVE HELLO

Needs: T-Stand
                Reward
                Cue and Bridge

 Lesson Time: 5-15 minutes depending on the bird's attention span

DESCRIPTION
The wave is a behavior in which the bird stands on one foot while waving up and down with the other, as if waving hello. This behavior is quickly learned, but you must be very quick with your bridge.

1 With your bird quietly perched on a T-stand, reach out your hand as if you want your bird to step onto it.

2 As soon as your bird lifts its foot, bridge and reward it. Do not allow the bird to get onto your hand.

3 Repeat step two, this time using a cue while offering your hand. As soon as your bird lifts its foot, bridge and reward it. While repeating the cue, gradually begin to move your hand farther and farther away from the bird until it cannot possibly reach your hand. Now your bird will begin to realize that you are bridging and rewarding it for picking up its foot.

4 With your hand back, give your cue while moving your hand up and down. The bird should try to follow your motion. Bridge and reward the bird when you see it begin to follow your up and down motion in addition to picking up its foot.

5 With your hand 5-8 inches away from the bird, wave while giving the cue. Delay the bridge and reward until the bird is mimicking the up and down motion fully.

6 With your hand further away (perhaps a foot), begin to decrease your waving motion to a finger waggle as you deliver the cue.

NOTE: For professional birds, you can slowly eliminate the verbal command. The finger waggle alone is an easily hidden cue mechanism. In case your bird begins to incorporate his behavior with his cue, use Hi, Hello, Hi There, or something similar. If your bird says a lot of Hello variations, use only a hand cue. The reason for this is so that the bird is not getting cued by people who know its vocabulary, without also being bridged and rewarded.

Remember the three elements to successful communication with your bird;

1. Be Consistent
2. Be Consistent
3. Be Consistent

GIVE A KISS

The kiss is a simple and fun behavior to teach a tame bird. This is the first trick your bird will learn while sitting on your hand. Take care to have the kiss consist of the bird's beak lightly touching your lips and not pinching or biting.

Needs: This trick will be performed with the bird perched on your hand.
Reward
Cue and Bridge

Remember to use a consistent bridge!

 Lesson Time: 5-15 minutes depending on the birds attention span

1 Place a reward between your teeth, let the bird see it. Keep another reward in your hand, also where the bird can see it. Using the treat in your hand, direct the bird to the treat between your teeth.

2 Allow the bird to take the treat from between your lips, bridge, and reward it with the treat in your hand.

3 Repeat the first two steps. Gradually eliminate signalling with the treat in your hand. Your bird will start to go for the treat in your lips on its own after a few rounds of this.

4 Once the bird is going toward the treat in your mouth on its own, cover the treat with your lips as the bird's beak makes contact. Bridge and reward the bird with the treat in your hand as soon as its beak contacts your lips. Don't allow the bird to take the treat from between your teeth.

5 Repeat step 4 several times. Next, eliminate the use of the treat between your teeth. Use the treat in your hand to direct the bird toward your lips as you give the verbal cue. As soon as the bird's beak contacts your lip, bridge and reward. Gradually decrease the motion of your hand until the bird is responding solely to the verbal cue.

NOTES: Do not cue the bird for a kiss without bridging and rewarding. It is terribly tempting to request a kiss behavior just for the fun of it. Do not reward the bird if it bites or pinches your lip, he should simply touch your lips with his beak.

NOD YES

Needs: T-Stand
           Reward
           Cue and Bridge

 Lesson Time: 5-15 minutes depending on the birds attention span

DESCRIPTION
Nodding Yes is another simple behavior you can teach your parrot to perform.

1 With the bird quietly perched, hold a treat between your fingers, just out of the bird's reach. Once the bird notices the treat, move your hand up and down while giving the cue for Nod Yes. As the bird begins to follow your hand motion with its head, bridge and reward it.

2 Gradually moving your hand farther away from the bird, repeat the cue. As the bird moves its head up and down, bridge and reward. As your hand moves farther away from the bird, it will begin to realize it is being rewarded for its nodding behavior.

3 Decrease the movement of your hand each time you repeat the trick, while giving the cue. You will eventually eliminate the hand cue altogether. At first, you will be rewarding the bird for any up or down motion of its head. Gradually increase your expectations until the bird bobs its head several times before being bridged and rewarded.

NOTE: Using a hand cue for this behavior means that you can use it in a show--occassionally asking the parrot questions and having it nod its head yes (or No--see next trick). Because the Nod Yes/Nod No/Wave Hello behaviors are very similar, cues for each behavior should be clearly distinct from one another.

NOD NO

Needs: T-Stand
              Rewards
              Cue and Bridge

 Lesson Time: 5-15 minutes depending on
the bird's attention span

DESCRIPTION
*Nodding No is another simple behavior to get your
parrot to perform, but it can be a little confusing to
some parrots who have just mastered yes. Be sure
that your verbal cues for Yes/No sound different.
This trick is virtually the same as Nod Yes.*

1   With the bird quietly perched hold a treat
between your fingers, just out of the bird's
reach. Once the bird notices the treat, move
your hand from side to side while giving the
cue for Nod No. As the bird begins to follow
your hand motion with its head, bridge and
reward it.

2   Gradually moving your hand farther away
from the bird, repeat the cue. As your hand
moves farther away, the bird will begin to
realize it is being rewarded for its behavior.

3 Decrease the movement of your hand while giving the cue, gradually eliminating the hand movement altogether. At first, you will reward the bird for any side to side motion of its head. Gradually, you will increase your expectations, until the bird shakes its head several times before being bridged and rewarded.

NOTE: You can also teach a bird this trick by placing a piece of tape on the back of the bird's head. The bird will try to shake the tape off, bridge and reward. Using a hand cue for this trick makes it very versatile. I like to begin a bird show with the question, "Do you know any tricks?" and have the bird vigorously nod its head No.

PARROT CARD TRICK

Needs: Deck of Cards
                     Cue
                     Bridge and Reward

 Lesson Time: 5-15 minutes depending on the bird's attention span

DESCRIPTION
This card trick takes advantage of the parrot's propensity for destroying things. The only difficult part of this trick is getting the card back from the bird before it is completely destroyed.

1 Fan a deck of cards in front of the bird and use the cue, "Pick a card." When the bird takes a card, let him take a bite out of it. Bridge and reward the bird.

2 Repeat step one until the bird quickly releases the card to get his reward. Do not wrestle the card away from the bird.

NOTE: This trick is great in a show. Place the disfigured card in the deck and then retrieve it, asking the parrot, "Is this your card?" To which the parrot vigorously Nods No.

INTERMEDIATE BEHAVIORS

A bird must understand the training process before progressing to the tricks in this section.

Begin the tricks in this section only after your bird has mastered hand-taming and two or more beginning tricks.

If your training process is still moving slowly try removing food bowls from your bird's cage for 1-2 hours before your sessions. A hungry bird will be more attentive.

DESCRIPTION

In this behavior, the bird spreads both of its wings and holds the pose for a few beats. The method for teaching this trick varies depending on whether or not the bird likes to be touched underneath its wings.

Talking birds can learn to say, "Look at the Eagle" or, "I'm an Eagle" while performing this trick.

Needs: T-Stand
            Reward
            Cue and Bridge

 Lesson Time: 10-20 minutes. This is an
intermediate behavior. Your bird should
master beginning behaviors before
attempting this.

IF THE BIRD ENJOYS BEING SCRATCHED UNDER ITS WINGS:

1 With the bird on a perch, use your index
fingers to scratch beneath its wings. As the
bird lifts its wings, bridge and reward.

2 Next, use a verbal cue just before you scratch
beneath the bird's wings. As the bird lifts its
wings, bridge and reward. Repeat 5-10 times.

3 Gradually eliminate the use of your fingers,
graduating to a verbal cue or hand signal.
The bird will gradually learn to lift its wings
when it sees or hears its cue.

IF THE BIRD OBJECTS TO BEING HANDLED BENEATH ITS WINGS:

1 With the bird perched calmly on your hand, tilt your hand while giving the verbal cue. The bird will spread its wings to regain its balance. As soon as the bird extends its wings, bridge and reward the bird.

2 Next, use a verbal cue just before you tilt your wrist. As the bird lifts its wings, bridge and reward. Repeat 5-10 times.

3 As you cue the bird, gradually decrease the tilt of your hand until it is completely eliminated. The bird will eventually open its wings in response to the cue alone.

Note: Using both a verbal and a hand cue for trick training allows you to gradually eliminate one of them, as you decide which is easier for you to use.

SHAKE HANDS

Needs: T-Stand
                      Reward
                      Cue and Bridge

 Lesson Time: Because it can confuse a newly hand tamed bird, this is an intermediate behavior. Wait until the bird is familiar with the training process before attempting this behavior. You can spend 10-20 minutes per session working on this behavior.

DESCRIPTION
Shaking hands is a behavior somewhat like waving hello. The bird stands on one foot while lightly grasping one of your fingers and moving it up and down, as if shaking hands. This behavior is usually quickly learned, but do not allow the bird to get onto your hand. The cue for this behavior must be very different from the one you use to get the bird onto your hand.

1   With your bird quietly perched, reach out your hand as if you want your bird to step onto it. Allow the bird to grasp one finger and begin shaking in a gentle up and down

motion, bridge and reward. (Do not let the bird get up onto your hand).

2 As soon as your bird replaces its foot on the T-stand, give the cue while offering your finger. Do not allow the bird to get onto your hand. Repeat the shaking gesture, bridge and reward. If you want to use a hand cue, begin to incorporate it with the trick at this stage. Birds have excellent eyesight and you can make the cue wiggling a single finger. A bird can differentiate this motion from that of being offered the side of your hand for perching.

3 Repeat step two 5-10 times and then cue the bird without offering your finger. The bird should pick up its foot and initiate the handshake. Bridge and reward. At this stage you can gradually eliminate the verbal cue if you desire.

LIGHTS OUT

Needs: Wall-mounted light switch
Reward
Cue and Bridge

 Lesson Time: 10-20 minutes. This is an intermediate behavior. Your bird should have mastered beginning behaviors before attempting this.

DESCRIPTION

In this behavior, the bird turns off the lights from a wall mounted switch. Many birds will discover this trick if their cage is close enough to a wall switch. But beware, if given enough time, a large parrot can chew through the insulation on the switch and electrocute itself.

1   With the bird perched calmly on your hand, place it in front of the wall switch. In no time the bird will grab the switch in its beak, bridge and reward.

2   Next, with the bird in front of the switch, use the cue you've chosen for Lights Out, and as the bird grabs the switch, bridge and reward.

3 With the bird watching, flip the switch on and off a few times. Once more, place the bird within reach of the switch and give the cue. As the bird grabs the switch, gently assist the bird in pulling it down by placing one finger on top of its beak and applying pressure. As soon as the light goes off, bridge and reward the bird.

4 Repeat step three 4-6 times, assisting the bird with moving the light switch. Gradually allow the bird to perform the behavior without help from you.

NOTE: This is a great way to get the kids to bed, especially if the bird says, "good night," "time for bed," or "bedtime!"

BANKER PARROT

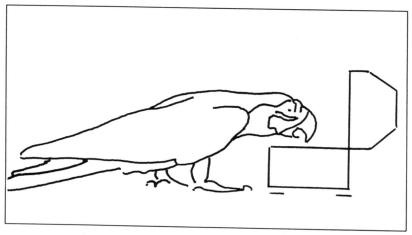

Needs: A table the bird can move around on.
          Rewards
          Quarters or Half Dollars
          Bowl and Piggybank
          Cue and Bridge

 Lesson Time: 10-20 minutes. This is an intermediate behavior. Your bird should have mastered beginning behaviors before attempting
this.

DESCRIPTION
*This behavior has a few steps to it, and it takes a
little patience to weave the various required
behaviors together. Birds love to place objects*

inside of other objects, and every bird I have tried this with has figured out the game. Most birds love this trick and will play this game on their own if given the props.

1 Prepare a table top with a few clean coins (not small coins that can be swallowed), and a cup or a bowl. Place the bird on the table and wait for him to pick up a coin and place it in the bowl, bridge and reward. Since you'll hear a loud noise when the coin drops, it isn't necessary to watch the bird closely.

2 Remove the coins from the table. Offer the bird a coin from your hand, and give the cue. When the bird drops the coin in the bowl, bridge and reward.

3 Repeat step two until the bird quickly takes its cue. Now, with the piggybank in front of the bird, drop a coin into the slot. Give a coin to the bird and cue. The bird will probably have a little difficulty with the slot at first, but with some practice, the bird will become adept at filling the bank.

BASKETBALL

Needs: **Table**
                     Bird Basketball Set
                     Reward
                     Cue and Bridge

 Lesson Time: 10-20 minutes. This is an intermediate behavior. Your bird should master beginning behaviors before you attempt this one.

DESCRIPTION

In this behavior, the bird picks up a specially designed basketball and lands it through a hoop. This trick can be taught in much the same way as the banking trick. NOTE: Two birds who get along well can be very entertaining "playing basketball" together. This is a terrific way to entertain visiting children.

1 Prepare a tabletop with the ball and basket. Place the bird on the table with the ball in front of him. As the bird picks up the ball, use the treat in your hand to direct the bird to the basket. As the bird approaches the basket, use the treat in your hand to direct the bird to place the ball in the basket. When the bird does place the ball in the basket, bridge and reward.

2 Next, hand the ball to the bird while giving the cue. Gradually decrease the direction that you give with the treat in your hand. When the bird drops the ball in the basket, bridge and reward.

3 Repeat step two until the bird is quickly taking the ball to the basket without being directed with its treat. Bridge and reward at the moment the bird releases the ball into the basket.

NOTE: Since birds are imitative you can speed up the learning process by setting an example. Before beginning the training session play with the basketball set, making baskets, while the bird is watching. Bird Basketball sets can be purchased from sources listed in the Supplier Index on page 93.

FETCH

Needs: Small, Indestructible Bird Toy
           Reward
           Cue and Bridge

 Lesson Time: 10-20 minutes. This is an
intermediate behavior. Your bird should
master a few beginning behaviors before
attempting this.

DESCRIPTION

*In this behavior, the bird learns to chase after
something you throw, and bring it back to you.
This can be a great way to make sure your parrot
gets plenty of exercise, and can be used in many
ways to build a show.*

*This behavior must be taught in several steps. First,
the bird must learn to drop something out of its
beak on cue. Second, it must learn to chase
something you throw. And third, it must learn to
return to you with the object.*

1 With the bird on a table, place the
object which you will use for this trick
in front of the bird. Let the bird play
with the object. When the bird releases

the object from its mouth, bridge and reward. Repeat 4-5 times.

2 The next time the bird picks up the object, give the cue to release. When the bird drops the object, bridge and reward. Repeat this step 5-10 times.

3 Show this same object to the bird and toss it a short distance. When the bird gets the object in its beak, use the cue for release. As the bird releases the object from its beak, bridge and reward. Repeat this step 5-10 times.

4 Throw the object, using the cue for Fetch. Gradually increase the distance the bird travels toward you before you bridge and reward. The bird will naturally return to you for its treat. Do not reward the bird for dropping the object and running back to you. At first meet the bird half way but then gradually increase your expectations until the bird is coming all the way back and dropping the object in front of you.

ADVANCED
BEHAVIORS

The behaviors in this section
require a high level of trust and
communication between bird and trainer. The
tricks in this section also require an understanding of the training process by your bird. Do not
attempt these tricks before mastering at least
two intermediate behaviors.

By this time you are becoming an accomplished
trainer and you will begin to notice subtle differ-
ences in the level of communication you share
with your bird. Allow what you know to enter
your training sessions!

DESCRIPTION

In this behavior, the bird gets onto and rides a specially designed bird toy such as a bicycle or skateboard. Most props come with instructions on how they should be used. Take care that your bird does not become terrified of the toy. Don't rush the bird into this behavior. If the bird reacts poorly to the toy, do not ruin your training relationship by pushing this or any other behavior on him.

Needs: Smooth Floor Surface
           Bird Skates, Bicycle, or other
           Riding Toy
           Reward
           Cue and Bridge

 Lesson Time: 15-20 minutes. This is an advanced behavior requiring a level of trust between bird and trainer.

1 With your bird on a smooth surface, coax it onto the riding toy from your hand. Be careful not to rush the bird. When the bird is on the toy, bridge and reward.

2 Allow the bird to get a grip with both feet and balance itself. As soon as the bird is balanced, assist the bird in moving the toy forward; bridge and reward.

3 Repeat steps one and two 5-10 times, adding the cue. Using the cue, gradually decrease the amount of assistance you give the bird with getting onto the toy. Bridge and reward the bird for getting onto the toy unaided.

4 Next, allow the bird to begin moving the toy forward on its own. At first, reward the bird for any forward momentum. Gradually increase your expectations by withholding the bridge and reward until the bird has ridden several feet on its own.

NOTE: Riding toys can be purchased from various sources listed in the Supplier Index on page 93. Some riding toys come with a training dowel which the bird can grasp with its beak. If the riding toy you purchase does not come with one, a tree branch will work just as well.

TALKING ON CUE

Needs: T-Stand
             Reward (This may simply be the
             chance to interact with you)
             Cue and Bridge

 Lesson Time: 15-20 minutes. This is an advanced behavior which requires that your bird understands the training process.

DESCRIPTION

Many, but not all, birds can be taught to talk on cue. Observe when your talking bird is most talkative and schedule your training sessions then. Do not reward a word that you did not cue. The bird will begin to repeat words or a single word incessantly, simply to get a treat.

1 During your bird's talkative time of day, place him on a perch in front of you. Let the bird see his treats and then give him his cue. A hand cue can be less confusing than a verbal cue. When you get the desired response, bridge and reward. If you do not want to use hand signals for your cue, using the word you want repeated is the simplest first lesson.

2

Repeat the process until the bird has firmly established that he is being rewarded for the proper response. When the bird is responding immediately with the desired word or phrase, move on to a new word or phrase.

3

When teaching a new word or phrase, two things must be done. First, ensure that all of the cues are clearly different from one another to avoid confusion. Second, reinforce the learned words or phrases by having the bird perform each one he knows at least once every other training session.

QUESTION/ANSWER TRAINING

Needs: T-Stand
An Assistant
Reward
Cue and Bridge

 Lesson Time: 15-20 minutes. This is an advanced behavior which requires that your bird understands the training process.

DESCRIPTION

Question/answer training is difficult, but it is highly rewarding. In this session, an assistant will be answering you in the way that you want the bird to (i.e., acting as a model for the behavior). Your bird must be familiar with the cue-bridge-reward sequence in order to learn this behavior quickly.

1. During your bird's talkative time of day, place him on a perch in front of you with an assistant standing beside him, facing you. Give a cue in the the form of a question (e.g., "How are you?") and have your assistant give the proper reply (e.g., "I'm fine"); bridge and pretend to reward your assistant. You may want to include a hand signal along with the verbal cue.

2 Repeat step one. Direct your attention and eye contact to the bird but have your assistant keep responding. When your assistant responds, direct your attention to him and ignore the bird.

3 After about 10 rounds with the assistant, try working with the bird alone. When the bird gives the proper reply, bridge and reward. Reinforce the behavior at least 4 times before ending the session. If possible, hold another training session later in the day. Never reward the bird for the wrong response.

NOTE: With patience, this type of training can be done without an assistant. You simply cue and wait for the desired response. Try structuring a cue around one of your bird's favorite words or phrases.

WHISPERING PARROT

Needs: T-Stand to start. Then progress
              to performing on the hand.
              Rewards
              Cue and Bridge

 Lesson Time: This trick is for any bird
whether it talks clearly or only makes
garbled noises. You can spend 10-20
minutes per session working on this trick.

DESCRIPTION
*The whisper is an adorable behavior to teach a bird.
It can be used in many ways when designing a show
for your bird. This trick is a combination of talking
on cue and the kiss behavior. Take care to have the
whisper consist of the bird's beak touching your ear
(not pinching or biting), and grumbling softly. This
trick has two steps. First the bird learns to make
low whispering noises on cue, and then he learns to
lean into your ear while doing so.*

1 During a time in the day when your bird is
talking softly or muttering to itself, bridge
and reward it for its behavior. Consistency of
the noise is not important, consistency of the
noise level is.

2 Graduate to using cues. I recommend using both verbal and hand cues for this behavior at first. Use the verbal cue until the bird mutters or mumbles something, bridge and reward.

3 Once the bird quickly responds to the verbal cue to mutter something, get the bird to sit calmly on your hand. As you show the bird the treat in your hand, direct it to lean into your ear while you cue the muttering behavior. It is not necessary to have the bird contact your ear--leaning into your ear works great. Once the bird mutters while leaning into your ear, bridge and reward. Repeat this step at least 10 times.

4 Now begin to decrease the amount of direction you give the bird with your hand, and gradually eliminate the verbal cue. The simplest cue to use is a hand wave or finger that you have adapted from the direction you were giving the bird to move towards your ear. Your final goal is to have the bird lean toward your ear and mutter, as a response to your hand cue.

TRAINING NATURAL BEHAVIORS

Needs: T-Stand
                Reward
                Bridge and Cue

 Lesson Time: 15-20 minutes. This is an advanced behavior which requires that your bird understands the training process.

DESCRIPTION
This is the way to condition any behavior that your bird already performs on his own. Conditioning will help him to perform it on cue. As you are watching your bird play, think of how you can incorporate its natural behaviors into unique tricks.

1 This training session will begin with your bird playing in its own environment, preferably an open playground. I'll use stretching as the sample behavior. As you observe the bird standing on one foot stretching its wing and leg, bridge and reward it. It will normally stretch the opposite side. Cue the bird just before you see it shifting its weight. As the bird goes into a stretch, bridge and reward.

2 Repeat step one the next few times you observe your bird stretching. Next, progress to the training area and give the cue. Be patient, repeating the cue, and mimicking the desired behavior if necessary. Bridge and reward the parrot as soon as it performs the behavior.

3 Reinforcement is crucial to conditioning natural behaviors. Be sure to have the bird perform these behaviors several times (two-to-four) in each training session. You may want to have an impromptu two-minute training session with your bird several times each day.

Natural behaviors can be incorporated into many performance routines. The above stretch can be incorporated into a magic show where the parrot gets to be the assistant sitting on the magician's shoulder. The cue is, "And my distinguished assistant Jaco!"

NOTE: Include a lot of conditioned, natural behaviors to formulate your parrot's own, unique routine. This is the easiest way to creates a distinctive and exciting show.

TABLE MANNERS

Needs: Metal Spoon
Honey
Piece of fruit, seed, or other small,
suitable food

 Lesson Time: This is a less structured training session. You do not need to worry about
abusing your bird's attention span here.

1 This is a trick your parrot may figure out for
itself. Use honey to get a small piece of the
parrot's favorite food to stick to a spoon. Let
the bird take the spoon handle in its claw.
The parrot will "spoon feed" itself within
minutes.

2 If the parrot doesn't initiate the behavior
with the food in its bowl, apply more honey
and dip the spoon in its feed dish.

NOTE: Do not allow your bird to eat at the table at mealtimes
unless you are prepared to always let it join you. The ruckus
created by a bird deprived of its dinner time with the family
will ruin any dinner party. As funny as this might sound, I've
met several parrot owners who've learned this lesson the hard
way.

ACROBATIC PARROT

Needs: This trick can be taught on a T-stand
          or from the hand.
          Bridge
          Cue and Reward

 Lesson Time: 5-10 minutes. This is an advanced behavior which requires a great deal of
trust from your bird.

DESCRIPTION

In this trick the bird hangs upside down on cue.
Most birds love to do this as long as they have trust
in their handler. Some birds will hang from one leg.
I say ,"Ta Da!" in the hope that a parrot will mimic
me. Some do.

1   With the parrot perched on your hand (on
     the T-stand is o.k.), show him his reward.
     Bring the hand with the reward in it down
     below the hand the parrot is perched on. As
     the bird reaches for the treat, move it further
     and further away, until the bird is upside
     down, bridge and reward. Repeat this step
     5-10 times.

2 Next, using the cue first, repeat step one. Again, when the bird is hanging upside down, bridge and reward. Repeat this step 5-10 times.

3 Gradually eliminate using the treat to get the parrot upside down. This can be done by hiding the treat from the bird while moving your hand in the same motion, and then by gradually decreasing the motion of your arm to nothing. Your final cue can be either verbal or a discreet finger waggle.

SLEEPY PARROT/PLAY DEAD

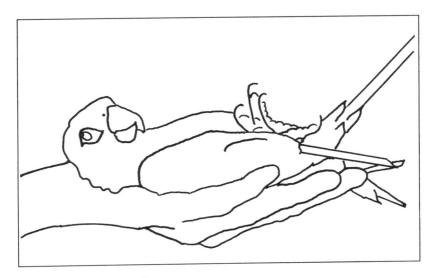

Needs: Bridge
            Cue
            Reward

 Lesson Time: 5-10 minutes. This is an advanced behavior which requires a great deal of trust from your bird.

DESCRIPTION
In this behavior, the bird will lie on its back at your command. Your bird must first become comfortable with lying on its back. Choose a time when things are quiet and the bird is in a trusting mood.

1 Sit down with the bird perched on your hand and gently turn it on its back. The easiest way to get a bird to lay on its back is to gently hold the bird against your chest and lean forward, using the hand the bird is not perched on as a cradle for its back and wings. Even the gentlest bird will probably grab your hand with its beak in an attempt to right itself. Reassure the bird until you can get it to lie somewhat still in your hand, bridge the bird, turn it gently upright and reward it.

2 Using the cue, turn the bird over onto its back. As the bird lies still for a moment, bridge, turn upright, and reward. Repeat step two several times.

3 When the bird is lying on its back, gently remove the bird's feet from the hand it was perched on. When the bird lies still for a few counts, bridge the bird, turn it upright, and reward. Repeat step three several times.

4 The hardest part of this behavior is to get the bird to release its feet from the hand it was perched on. Cupping your free hand, gently cover the bird's head, then lift and tilt the hand the bird is perched on. In essence you are "dumping" the bird into your free hand. When the bird is upside down, wiggle your hand out of its clutches. As soon as the bird releases your hand, bridge, wait 4 counts, turn the bird upright, and reward. The final goal is to have the bird obediently accept being turned upside down, releasing its grip on your hand without a struggle, and laying still for a few beats.

NOTE: Be very careful! If your bird panics, bites you, and then ends up on the floor, he will never like this trick. Conditioning this trick is largely a matter of trust building. Never perform it carelessly.

GETTING WORK FOR YOUR PERFORMING PET

Depending on where you live, you can make your trained pet available to film makers, ad agencies, or as entertainment at special events. If you live near a major metropolitan area, call a local talent agency and ask if they will represent a trained bird.

If you have no luck finding an agent, there will probably be a nearby film-makers' resource agency listed in the yellow pages. Ask your local reference librarian for help in tracking it down.

REQUIREMENTS

Performing animals must be in top physical condition--no feather plucking or chewed tail feathers. When clipping your bird's wings, leave the two outermost primary feathers intact. This will create a smoother line, while still keeping your bird safe.

Performing animals must be reliable. Imagine showing up for the filming of a commercial, where it is costing the advertisers thousands of dollars per hour to shoot, and finding that your bird is reluctant to perform under the lights. Take a few test runs in a busy area before accepting any paid assignments.

The rate you can charge for a performing animal varies greatly depending on where you live and the medium in which the animal will be used. A steadily performing animal can make a healthy income by anyone's standards, especially if it is used repeatedly for television commercials.

If your bird is an exceptional performer, I recommend pursuing a talent agent. If there is not a talent agent in your area who is willing to handle animals, send information on your pet to local advertising agencies--to the attention of the Creative Director. The Creative Director oversees the creation of ad campaigns, and your pet may give him some inspiration. If you can afford it, use video tape. If not, at least include a photo and a detailed description of your pet's unique qualities and behavior.

If you would like to provide entertainment for fairs, special events and children's parties, contact local caterers and party planners. Arrange to show them your bird's act, set an agreeable hourly rate, and tell them how to contact you. Most party planners will charge more to their clients than they pay you, and that's standard. If you want to find your own clients, put an ad in local newspapers and the yellow pages.

SAMPLE PET RESUME

LUCIANO PARROTTI

Species:
Congo African Grey

Special Qualities:

This bird has an exceptional speaking voice and quickly learns new phrases. He will perform simple behaviors such as nodding his head, waving, bowing, and playing dead. Has performed reliably in public and on camera numerous times.

New behaviors will be trained on request, with two weeks advance notice.

WHAT TO INCLUDE
For this bird I would include a Black and White glossy photograph, taken at a professional portrait studio (such as Sears--they'll get a real kick out of it!), and an audio cassette that is humorously narrated and demonstrates the bird's speaking voice. Just remember, trick-trained birds are amusing. Make your bird's promotional package the highlight of somebody's day.

PUTTING TOGETHER A SHOW

Your bird's personality and talents will dictate how you will structure a bird show. A talking bird is a fascinating animal and this ability should always be highlighted in a show. A beautiful bird is wonderful to see and touch. If your bird is a colorful one, make sure to teach it The Eagle so that you can show off its plumage. Even in a rural area where you may not get any high-paying commercial work, you can earn money entertaining children at birthday parties or fairs.

Putting together a show with a trained bird is one of my favorite parts of behavior conditioning and trick training. I encourage you to condition your bird to perform any of its unique behaviors on cue and incorporate these into your show.

Below is a script for a show featuring a talking bird who knows Nod Yes, Nod No, The Eagle, Give a Kiss, Acrobatic Parrot, Sleepy Parrot/Play Dead, Bowing, and Talking on Cue.

Handler: Hi, my name's Jennifer and this is Parrotman. (Yep, that's the bird's name)
    The bird, perched on the handler's shoulder, extends one wing and foot, as if bowing, and

says, "Ta Da!" The handler removes the bird
from her shoulder and places it on a T-stand.

Handler: Well Parrotman, do you want to do some
tricks for these people?

Parrotman vigorously Nods No.

Handler: Well, would you like some treats?

Parrotman vigorously Nods Yes.

Handler: O.K. then, would you just tell everyone
what kind of bird you are.

Parrotman performs The Eagle declaring,
"I'm an Eagle!"

Handler picks up Parrotman and says, "Someone
must have fed you goof loops! You're not an
Eagle."

Parrotman hangs upside down from the
handler's hand and says, "I feel fine." Upright
on the handler's arm, Parrotman performs
sleepy parrot.

Handler: Well, I'm afraid Parrotman is too tired to
go on.

Parrotman gets up and performs Whispering
Parrot.

Handler: Oh, Parrotman says it's Sarah's 5th
birthday, and he wants to give her a birthday kiss.

When the child gets up, show the child how to

properly hold the bird and how to cue the bird to give a kiss. The handler will immediately take the bird back; bridge and reward.

End of show.

NOTES: You'll notice that this show is not very long. A single parrot will not perform for any extended period of time (more than 10 minutes) without becoming soured to perfoming. Most bird shows feature several birds who each perform for less than 5 minutes. You can stretch the show by introducing your bird and giving some background on its exceptional qualities. If you are looking toward Movies or T.V. you will want to train several identical birds the same behaviors.

To prepare for the "big time" ask friends and relatives to act as an audience while you "dress rehearse" your parrot. If you can't get a ready audience, go to a park or shopping center and put your bird through its paces. Parrots need time to adjust to new places, sights and sounds and it's a good idea to take a performing bird out in public as much as possible during the training phase. You'll probably draw a crowd!

Afterword

I hope this book has been enjoyable and understandable. If you are training your bird to be a movie star I hope you'll remember me on Johnny Carson. If you are training your bird to channel its energy and to build a closer relationship (as I do), I know you'll be pleased with the results of your efforts.

I have named my house The Warshaw Home For Wayward Parrots. I can never resist a challenge, and "problem" birds are constantly being given away by well-meaning but mis-informed owners who cannot deal with these perplexing creatures. I hope this book saves you from showing up at my front door (Hmmm . . . maybe we could get rid of the refrigerator and put another cage there).

Your bird has amazing potential, and I hope I have helped you uncover some of the reasons why he does what he does. You needn't be an exceptional animal handler to succeed. If you can be patient, creative, and know how to set rules that both you and your birds can live with, then you are on your way! Bon Voyage.

SUPPLIERS INDEX

The following suppliers manufacture props for training parrots. Inclusion in this list does not represent endorsement for the products offered. Contact the suppliers for their product catalogs.

K.B. Specialty Products, Inc., P.O. Box 127, Park Rapids, Minnesota 56470
Suppliers of Roller Skates with training dowels.
Planning scooters and bicycles as of 1/6/90.
Phone 218/732-4171.

Parrot Mountain   Ocean, New Jersey
Suppliers of Roller Skates and Scooters.
Phone 1-800/362-8183 and 1-908/918-0266

Did You Borrow This Copy?

Additional copies can be ordered from:

Parrot Press
767 A Schiele Avenue
San Jose, CA 95126   408/297-7734

Single copies are $14.95 (includes $3 S&H). Foriegn Orders
please add $2 for shipping. California orders add local sales
tax of .87¢.

Multiple Order Discounts
call for current discount prices 408/297-7734.